DISCOVERING CANADA

The Railways

ROBERT LIVESEY & A.G. SMITH

Stoddart Kids

**We acknowledge the Canada Council for the Arts and the Ontario Arts
Council for their support of our publishing program.**

Published in Canada in 1997 by Stoddart Kids,
a division of Stoddart Publishing Co. Limited
34 Lesmill Road
Toronto, Canada M3B 2T6
Tel (416) 445-3333 Fax (416) 445-5967
E-mail Customer.Service@ccmailgw.genpub.com

Canadian Cataloguing in Publication Data

Livesey, Robert, 1940–
      The railways

(Discovering Canada series)
Includes index.
ISBN 0-7737-5901-8

1. Railroads – Canada – History –
Juvenile literature. I. Smith, A. G. (Albert Gray), 1945–   II. Title. III. Series:
Livesey, Robert, 1940–   Discovering Canada.

HE2808.L58 1997   j385′.0971   C97-930875-5

Printed and bound in Canada

Dedicated with love to
Lewis V. Watkins
and
Cousins Catherine and Joey

A special thanks to Richard McQuade, Josie Hazen, the librarians at the Oakville Public Library, the Sheridan College Library, the University of Windsor Library , Stephen Lyons, CP Archives, Garry Ness, Acadia University, and Sheila Dalton.

Other books in the Discovering Canada series

The Vikings

The Fur Traders

New France

Native Peoples

The Defenders

Contents

Introduction

Canada is the second largest country* in the world. It stretches from the Atlantic Ocean in the east to the Pacific Ocean in the west and from the U.S.A. border in the south to the Arctic Ocean in the north.

From the earliest times, transportation across the huge North American continent was a problem. Natives and early explorers used canoes and boats on the millions of inland rivers and lakes during the summer season, but in the Canadian north were reduced to snowshoes and dog-sled teams in the winter. Although Europeans had brought horses to North America, they were not a very effective means of transportation on dense, snow-covered forest trails.

When the steam engine was invented, it drastically changed the nature of transportation in the entire world, but especially in Canada. Samuel Cunard of Halifax, Nova Scotia was the first in the world to power a fleet of ocean ships by steam. The arrival of steam locomotives that could cross the North American continent by land in all seasons altered the nature of life in Canada completely.

* Canada: 9,970,000 square km; Russia: 17,075,000 square km

In the early 1850s, before the railways, Canada was a large country with a sparse population scattered in small towns and communities separated by long distances, rugged forests, rocky terrain, endless flat prairies, and high mountain ranges. There were no cars or highways; the idea of people being able to fly across the skies was beyond anyone's imagination at that time.

As the train tracks were laid across the country from the Atlantic to the Pacific, bustling new towns overflowing with settlers sprang up along the railway. The train station became the centre of life and information. The telegraph lines hummed with news from the outside world; notices were posted for all to read and the arrival of a train was an exciting event. The jobs created by building the railway brought money and business activity to these towns. The communication line made all Canadians feel united as a nation, helping to bring about the creation of the independent Dominion of Canada by 1867.

Railroad Language

Gauge means the width between the rails.

Standard Gauge (1.44 m) was used in the U.S.A. and later by the Canadian Pacific Railway. It is the gauge in use today.

Provincial Broad Gauge (1.67 m) was used at first in Canada West (Ontario) due to fear of American invasion, as it would prevent U.S. trains that ran on standard gauge from entering Canadian territory.

Narrow Gauge was the only gauge used in Newfoundland, Prince Edward Island and the Yukon. Today some mines and quarries still use it. It's cheaper to construct but trains move more slowly and carry lighter loads.

Crossties (Rail Ties) are the squared wooden timbers (2.59 m long) on which the rails are placed.

Spikes are made of steel and, when hammered into place, they secure the rails and crossties.

Rails are the metal tracks on which the train's wheels run. Iron rails, used at first, were less expensive than steel rails, but not as strong. Only steel is used today.

Fishplates are flat pieces of steel that link each rail to the next.

Laying Track is an assembly line of activity involving several different gangs and crews of workers.

Railroad Bed is the solid flat surface of crushed stone which has to be prepared before the tracks can be laid on it.

Sections of track run from one point to another and can vary in length.

End of Steel means the end of the tracks (construction progress to date).

Highball meant "proceed." Before signal lights were invented, a large ball raised to the top of a signal mast with a rope and pulley indicated a clear track ahead.

Sidings are side tracks built beside the main tracks at certain points so that trains can stop or wait for another train to pass them.

Young Hero

Tom, age twelve, sold newspapers and candy from early morning until midnight on the Grand Trunk Railway as the train travelled between Port Huron and Detroit. In 1859, it was common for boys to be working at such an early age as "candy butchers."

Tom's inquisitive mind got him in trouble when his secret experiments in the baggage car erupted into a phosphorous fire, and a later accident, when jumping onto a moving train left him half deaf. But he was so well-liked, that the train crew allowed the boy to drive the powerful locomotive at night, so that they could sleep.

Tom's life changed in 1862 when three-year-old Jimmie Mackenzie wandered onto the tracks at Mt. Clemens, Michigan, in front of an approaching train. Tom sprang to the rescue and pulled the child to safety

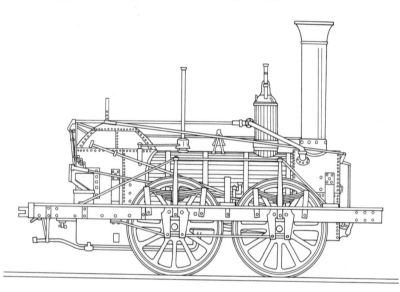

as the locomotive roared past. The grateful father was the stationmaster and rewarded fifteen-year-old Tom by teaching him to be a telegrapher.

For the next two years, Tom worked as a telegrapher at Stratford Junction, Ontario, where his interest in elementary circuitry grew. He discovered and implemented many technological advances in the fields of electricity, telegraphy, and sound recording. We remember him today as Thomas Edison, the inventor of the light bulb.

The First Railway

First Steam Locomotives
The first steam-driven locomotion railway in the world was George Stephenson's Stockton to Darlington line in Britain in 1825. Before then

railway cars had been pulled along tracks by teams of horses. The first Canadian use of steam was in 1830 at Cape Diamond, Quebec, during the construction of the Quebec Citadel. The steam-driven cable cars on tracks carried granite blocks up the steep hill.

The Champlain & St. Lawrence Railroad (C&St. L) 1836
Canada's first railroad, the Champlain & St. Lawrence, opened for business on July 21, 1836. It replaced 145 km of riverboat passage with 24 km of tracks from the steamboat wharf at Laprairie, Quebec, to St. John (St. Jean), Quebec. Its British-built locomotive, the *Dorchester* (0-4-0) had four large 7.62 cm wooden driving wheels and was nicknamed "the Kitten" because it was so skittish. The tracks were also made of wood (pine), with strips of iron on top.

Canada's First Railway Accident 1837
In the summer of 1837, a train on the Champlain & St. Lawrence Railroad was derailed when it hit a team of oxen crossing the tracks.

The Albion Railway (AR) 1838
Canada's second railroad was the Albion Colliery Tramway (later the Albion Railway) which carried coal about 10 km from the Nova Scotia mines to Pictou Harbour. Two of its original locomotives, the *Sampson* and the *Albion* (0-6-0) are preserved and on display in Nova Scotia today. They were the first locomotives on the North American continent to burn coal.

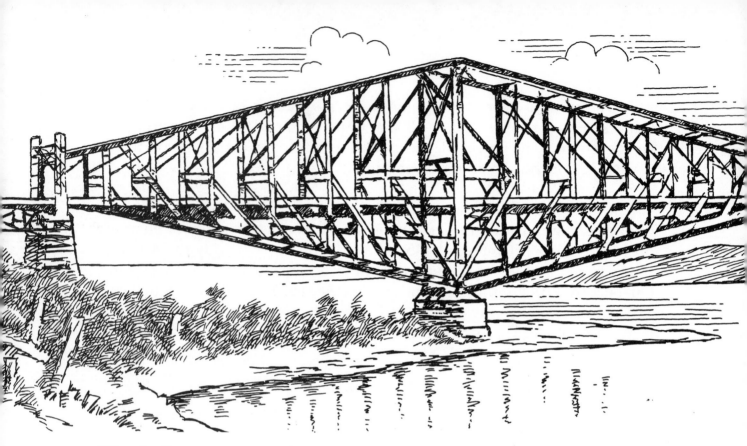

The St. Lawrence & Atlantic Railroad (St. L&A) 1852

This was the first international railway. It was called the Atlantic & St. Lawrence (A&St. L) in the U.S.A. and it linked Longueuil, near Montreal, to the ice-free port of Portland, Maine, on the Atlantic Ocean. It was immediately leased (for 999 years) by the Grand Trunk, a pioneer railway in Canada.

First Canadian Built Locomotive (OS&HR) 1853

The *Toronto* No. 2 of the Ontario, Simcoe & Huron Railroad (later the Northern Railway of Canada) was built in Toronto in 1853 by James Good. It is commemorated by a brass plaque at Toronto's Union Station.

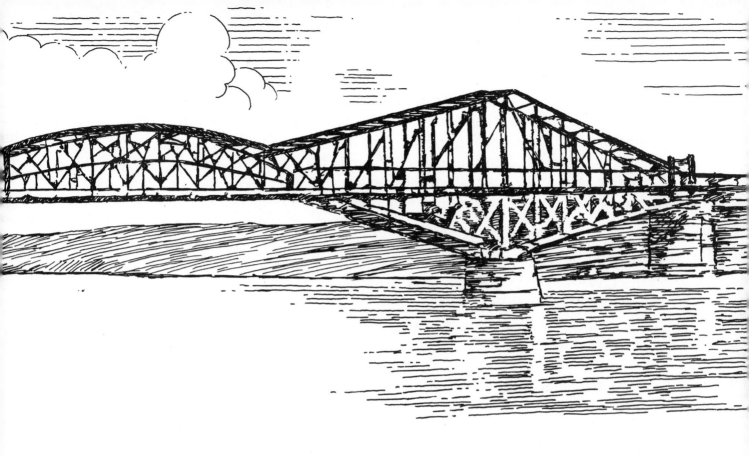

Eighth Wonder of the World 1859

The Victoria Tubular Bridge across the St. Lawrence River at Montreal was called the "Eighth Wonder of the World" when it was completed in 1859. It was a 2,010 m long rectangular iron tube that weighed 8,205 tonnes. Although it had openings in its rod, temperatures inside often reached 250° C on hot summer days. Because of its length and engineering, it was considered an international engineering marvel of its day. It was replaced in 1898 by the Victoria Jubilee Bridge, which is still in use today.

First Railroad Suspension Bridge (GWR) 1855

The first railroad suspension bridge was built by the Great Western Railway in 1855. Crossing the Niagara River at the famous Niagara Falls, it was a daring engineering marvel. It carried trains on an upper deck while pedestrians and carts used the lower deck. It was 260 m long, and 24,140 km of wire were used for suspension cables.

North America's First Attempted Train Robbery (GWR) 1856

On June 27, 1856, two desperadoes were removing a rail on the mainline of the GWR near Mosa Station, 53 km west of London, Ontario, in order to derail and rob a passenger train. But a track inspector surprised them, and the robbery was prevented. Although the men shot the inspector, he later recovered from his wounds.

First International Submarine Tunnel 1891

When it was completed in 1891, the St. Clair Tunnel connecting Sarnia, Ontario, with Port Huron, Michigan, was an engineering feat without parallel. It was the first time that two countries were connected by a tunnel bored under a riverbed. It continued to be used until April 1995 when a new tunnel was opened to replace it.

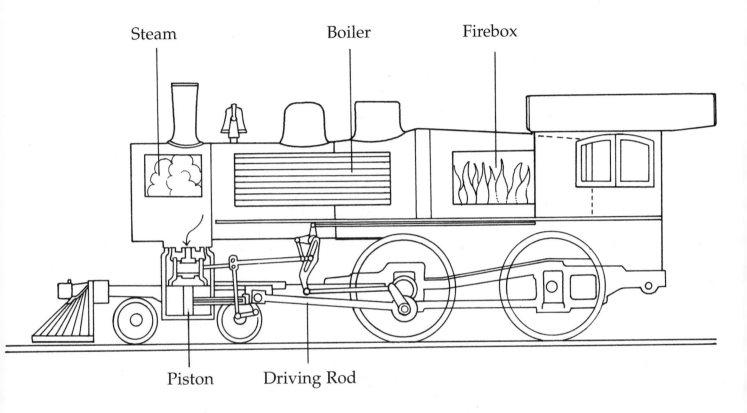

Steam   Boiler   Firebox

Piston   Driving Rod

How a Steam Locomotive Works

Steam engines work much like tea kettles. Water is heated in a boiler to
create steam. The steam expands into cylinders containing pistons which
in turn push driving rods. These rods are connected to and turn the large
driving wheels.

Train Crews

Conductor: The conductor is the boss on the train, the person who is in complete authority, much like the captain of a ship.

Porter: Traditionally, black people were porters on Canadian trains because, for many years, it was one of the few jobs open to them. Porters work on sleeping cars, welcoming the passengers, showing them to their seats, looking after their needs, and making up the beds.

Chief Steward, Waiters and Cooks: If the train has a dining car, the chief steward is in charge and supervises the cooks who prepare the meals, and the waiters who serve the passengers.

Brakeman: The brakeman is in charge of the train's brakes and responsible for bringing the train to a stop. The brakeman couples and uncouples cars when they are being switched in yards and at sidings.

Engineer: The engineer is the person who drives the locomotive that pulls the train along the tracks.

Fireman: The fireman was the person who shovelled the coal into trains pulled by steam locomotives so that the train continued to run. Firemen are no longer needed on modern trains.

11

The Roundhouse was where steam locomotives were serviced after each run. Some are still in use today. They were round because the tracks ran off a turntable or bridge which revolved in a circular pit, turning locomotives to face a different direction or sending them to individual stalls in the roundhouse.

12

Build a model locomotive

The earliest locomotives were quite simple. The engine was a steam engine on wheels with a platform on the rear for the engineer and fireman to stand. The attached tender supplied the fuel. Follow these instructions carefully to build your own locomotive.

What you need:

scissors   white glue
crayons or coloured pencils   scoring tool

What to do:

1. Photocopy pages 15 & 17.
    Colour the parts before cutting them out. Do not colour the tabs.
    colour suggestions:
    • body of boiler — brown with yellow (brass) fittings
    • ends of boiler and smoke stack — dark gray
    • wheels — dark red and black
    • tender body and wheels — dark red
    • wood — brown

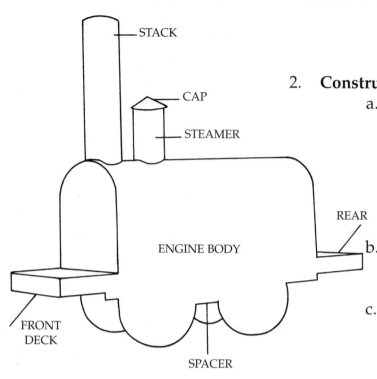

STACK

CAP

STEAMER

REAR

ENGINE BODY

FRONT DECK

SPACER

2. **Constructing the engine:**
   a. Cut out the engine body, and the front and rear decks. Score along the edges of the tabs and glue the engine body together. **Caution**: Apply glue only to the tabs. Do not use too much or it will seep through the paper and spoil it.
   b. After the engine body has dried, assemble the front and rear decks and glue them in place.
   c. Assemble the spacer and glue it out of sight between the sides of the engine body.

3. **The tender:**
   a. Assemble the tender body.
   b. Assemble the rim and glue it to the top of the tender.
   c. Assemble the spacer and glue it out of sight between the sides of the tender body.

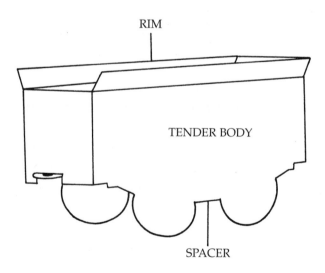

RIM

TENDER BODY

SPACER

14

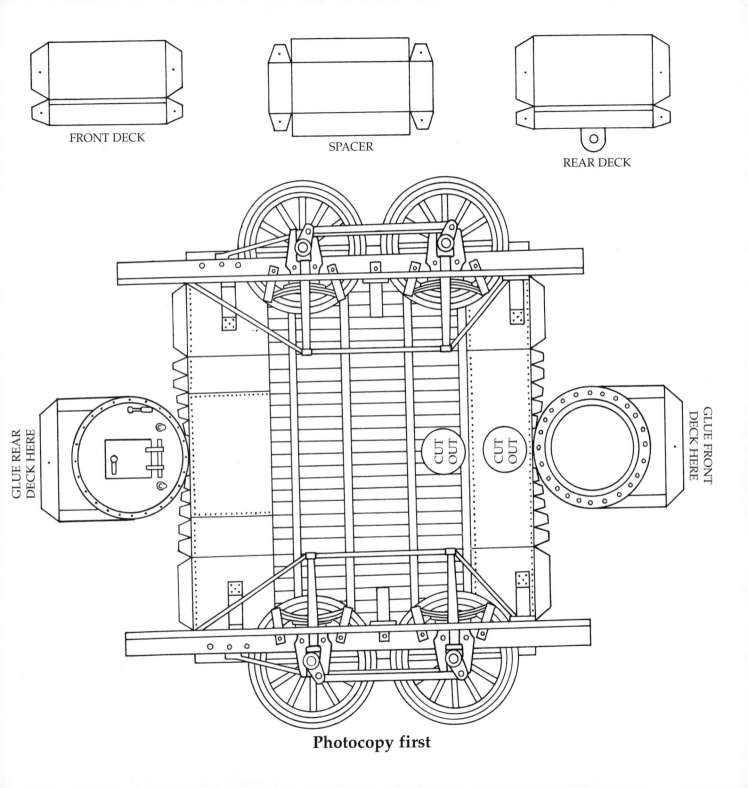

FRONT DECK

SPACER

REAR DECK

GLUE REAR DECK HERE

GLUE FRONT DECK HERE

CUT OUT

CUT OUT

Photocopy first

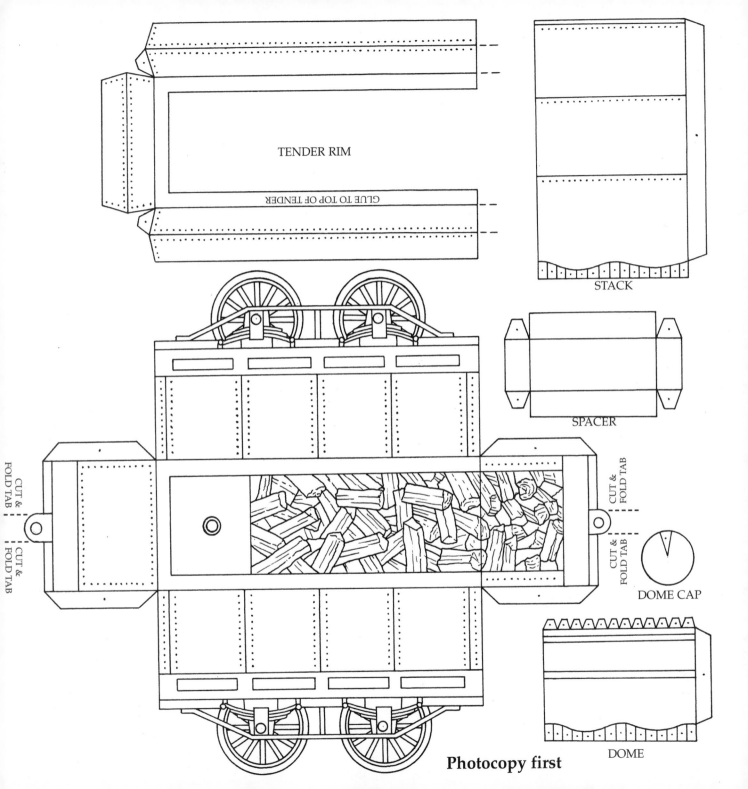

TENDER RIM

GLUE TO TOP OF TENDER

STACK

SPACER

CUT & FOLD TAB

CUT & FOLD TAB

CUT & FOLD TAB

CUT & FOLD TAB

DOME CAP

DOME

Photocopy first

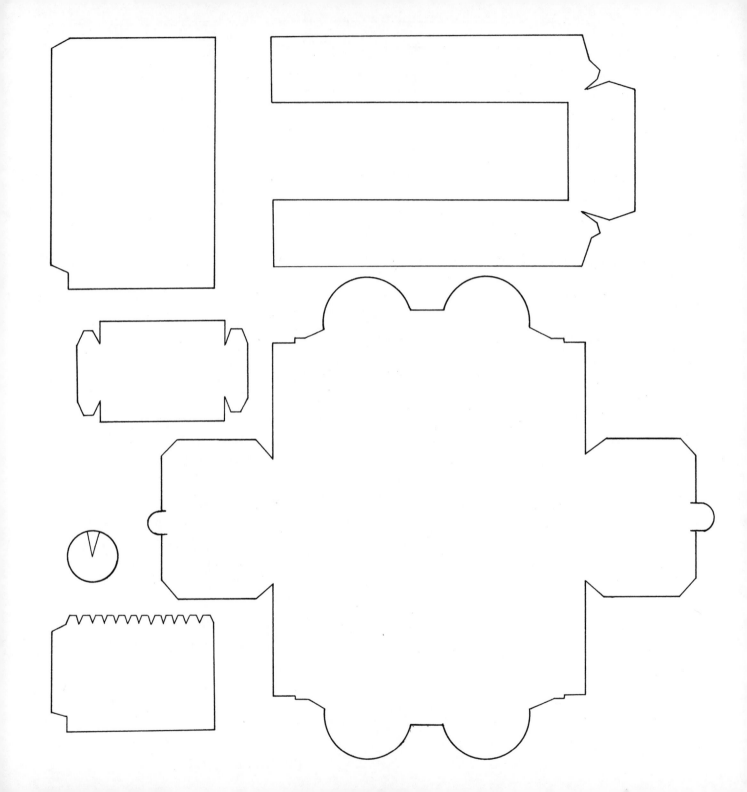

Sandford Fleming and Others

Before any railways could be built in Canada, someone had to travel through the unknown forests, paddle down the wilderness rivers, cross the endless plains, and hike through the tall mountains to decide on the best route that the future railroad might take.

These people, called surveyors, were trained to discover the shortest and safest way to construct railways across the vast Canadian territories. They had the lifestyle of a fur trader, living in tents, braving the heat and mosquitoes in the hot summers, enduring the freezing ice and snow in winter, and frequently hunting and fishing for their food as they went. At the same time they were educated scientists, trained in astronomy, mechanics and drafting, who used the latest instruments and tools to mark and record the directions and routes that the trains would take.

One of Canada's most famous surveyors was Sandford Fleming who was born on January 7, 1827, in Kirkcaldy, Scotland. As a youngster, Sandford, as well as his five brothers and two sisters, would often venture down to the harbour to view the tall wooden sailing ships that had come from all corners of the globe. Their grandfather had sailed on one of those vessels to fight with General Wolfe on the Plains of Abraham. Perhaps that was what attracted Sanford and his brother David to Canada.

Because Sandford was a natural artist and liked mathematics, he was apprenticed, at age fourteen, to train as a surveyor. In 1845, Sandford and David sailed to Canada on one of the tall ships to make their fortunes in the new land.

Within two years, the entire Fleming family had followed the two boys to Canada and settled on the Humber River near Toronto. In 1849, Sandford went to Montreal to take the examinations to become a provincial land surveyor.

North to Georgian Bay

In 1852, the red-bearded Fleming struggled across swamps, dense bush, and hard granite to survey one of Ontario's first railways, the Ontario, Simcoe & Huron Railroad, from Toronto to the shores of Georgian Bay. Sandford described the rough life of a surveyor as follows:

> It is one of the misfortunes of the profession to which I am proud to belong that our business is to make and not to enjoy; we no sooner make a rough place smooth than we move to another — leaving others to enjoy what we have accomplished.

21

The Intercolonial Railway

In 1863, Fleming was called to Quebec by the premier of the colony of Canada, John Sandfield Macdonald (not to be confused with Sir John A. Macdonald, the first prime minister of Canada). The colonial governments of New Brunswick, Nova Scotia, and Canada, along with the British government, had decided to build a railway connecting the provinces and all agreed that Sandford Fleming should be the surveyor.

In March of 1867, Fleming had completed the Truro-Pictou Railway in Nova Scotia. His new job was to discover the best route for the Intercolonial Railway.

Fleming and his survey crew travelled by dog sled and on snowshoes through the wilderness of New Brunswick, hunting everything from porcupines to moose for food along the way. In total, Fleming surveyed fifteen different routes before recommending a northern passage along the Baie de Chaleur for the Intercolonial tracks.

When the British colonies united on July 1, 1867, to form the independent Dominion of Canada, section 145 of the British North American Act stated that the building of an Intercolonial Railway was to begin within six months. On July 6, 1876, after nine years of construction, the first through train on the Intercolonial arrived in Quebec City from Halifax.

The Canadian Pacific Railway

While he was still working on the Intercolonial Railway, Fleming was given a second job by his friend, Prime Minister John A. Macdonald. A transcontinental railway had to be built to link the new province of British Columbia on the west coast with those in the east. Fleming quickly had twenty-one survey crews (more than 800 men) at work. Some came east from Victoria; others went west from the Ottawa River.

West to the Red River

As early as 1858, Fleming was giving public speeches about his dream of a railway stretching from coast to coast inside Canadian territory. But at that time the Northwest was controlled by the British-owned Hudson's Bay Company, which had a fur trading monopoly in what was then called Rupertsland.

In 1863, Fleming presented the Red River colonists' petition for a railway to the prairies to the premier of United Canada. He then travelled to Britain where he persuaded the Colonial Secretary to promise to release the control of the Northwest from the Hudson's Bay Company.

In 1878, the first train finally arrived on the Canadian prairies when the Pembina branch line linked Winnipeg to the Canadian Pacific Railway progressing from the east.

Kicking Horse Pass

Laying tracks across the vast prairies was a challenge, but blasting tunnels through the Rocky Mountains was an almost impossible task. Fleming surveyed and recommended the Yellowhead Pass route along the Thompson and Fraser Rivers, where the early fur traders had first found their way to the Pacific coast. When an American businessman, William Van Horne, took over the Canadian Pacific Railway Project, he was looking for short cuts and expediency and favoured Kicking Horse Pass, discovered by an American surveyor, Major A.B. Rogers.

The Last Spike

On November 7, 1885, the railway construction crews approaching from the east and west met at Eagle Pass in the middle of the Rocky Mountains. The railway owners arrived on a train from the east, and the last spike was hammered into place at Craigellachie, British Columbia, by Donald Smith, the senior director of the CPR. Sandford Fleming, by then a director, described the "spontaneous cheer" that erupted from "the pent up feelings" of the crowd witnessing the historical moment. On June 28, 1886, the first train left Montreal and travelled to the Pacific coast in only 140 hours, a trip that had taken the surveyor, Sandford Fleming, 103 days.

Almost Buried Alive

Kicking Horse Pass was given its name when an early explorer, James Hector, was kicked so hard by his horse that his native guides thought he was dead. When he awoke, he was in his grave and his helpers were preparing to bury him.

First Postage Stamp

It was Sandford Fleming who designed Canada's first postage stamp, the Threepenny Beaver, issued in 1851.

Message in a Bottle

When young Sandford Fleming and his brother sailed to Canada to seek their fortunes in 1845, their ship, the *Brilliant*, ran into a fierce storm in the middle of the dangerous Atlantic Ocean. As waves crashed over the ship, Sandford heard the wooden beams cracking and thought that he would certainly die. Desperately, he scribbled a farewell letter to his parents, placed it in a bottle and tossed the bottle into the raging sea.

Seven months later, after the boys had arrived safely in Canada, a

fisherman on the Devon coast in Britain found the bottle washed ashore and delivered it to Sandford's father, Andrew Fleming, in Kirkcaldy.

Standard Time

In 1876, while visiting Britain, Sandford Fleming found himself stranded at a railroad station for twelve hours because the departure time of his train read "5:35 a.m." rather than "5:35 p.m." Frustrated, he spent the time devising a new system of calculating time that used twenty-four hours a day rather than two twelve-hour segments.

In those days, every country and community in the world had different local times, and travellers were frequently confused. Using the lines of longitude as a guide, Fleming created twenty-four time zones thus making it possible for the entire world to be based on one standard time. When he announced his concept to the world, the Czar of Russia was one of the first to accept the idea. In October, 1884, twenty-five countries met in Washington, D.C. to agree on using the Greenwich Observatory in London, England as the standard against which all the clocks in the world would be set. Railways in Canada and the United States had adopted Fleming's Standard Time a year earlier.

Pacific Cable

His great patriotism for the British Empire of the late 1800s prompted Fleming to take on another challenge — convincing the governments of all the British colonies that they should construct a telegraph cable under the Pacific Ocean to link them together. He had always built telegraph lines along his railway tracks; now he set out to link the world together. Sir John A. Macdonald supported him, and by October 31, 1902, the Pacific Cable was in operation from Canada to Fiji, New Zealand and Australia.

The Workers

Navvies, Gangs, and Crews
Many different kinds of people helped to build the railways in Canada. They did not become famous, but without their hard work and dedication the Canadian railroads would not have been completed.

First, the **surveyors** travelled through the thick forests, across barren plains, and into deep mountain passes to decide on and mark the "trial line" or route for the railroad. They cut notches into trees or scraped symbols on rock faces as they progressed.

Grading gangs followed the path marked by the survey-ors, cutting down trees and clearing the route.

27

Measuring gangs arrived next with a chain 30.5 m long. They measured a chain length and then pounded a numbered stake into the ground that indicated the distance from their starting point.

Then **transit crews** used an instrument called a transit to calculate distances on curves, around lakes, or across high mountains.

Next, **levelling gangs** utilized another instrument, called a railway level, to calculate the height above sea level along the trial line. They left a "bench mark" every half mile that indicated the elevation through the hills and valleys.

Following the levellers came **topographers** who recorded information about the physical conditions that existed 30.5 m on each side of the trial line. They indicated such things as rivers, mountains, swamps, the kind of soil or rock, etc.

Once the route had been measured and recorded, the construction workers, called **navvies**, arrived to build a solid roadbed on which the trains would travel. The navvies used picks to create drainage ditches, and shovels to pack down two layers of crushed stone, called sub-ballast and ballast, that were hauled to the location by teams of horses and wagons.

When they were finished, horses dragged a giant scraper across the surface of the ballast to make it flat for the laying of the rails.

Once the roadbed was completed, **track layers** placed wooden timbers called ties 61 cm apart and laid two steel rails on top of them. The rails were secured to the ties with fishplates, and spikes were hammered into place to secure them all together.

The **bridge gangs** worked round the clock in shifts to build bridges over rivers or trestles across deep mountain valleys.

Dynamite crews blasted routes through the hard granite of Northern Ontario and the Rocky Mountains in British Columbia.

29

Make a Surveyor's Transit

In order for the surveyors to plan and lay out the routes of the railways, it was necessary to use a transit. Follow these instructions to make your own.

What you need:

> A small compass — 4 or 5 cm in diameter
> A piece of wood, 3 cm thick and 24 cm square
> A wooden dowel 1 cm thick
> A plastic drinking straw
> Small nails, thread, white glue
> A compass saw, a drill, a ruler

What to do:

1. Lay out and cut a wooden disc 20 cm in diameter. In the centre of this disc, cut a hole the diameter of your compass and glue it in place.
2. Lay out and cut the two vertical supports. Draw dials on the supports and drill a 1 cm hole in the centre.
3. Glue and nail the vertical supports to the base.
4. Cut out the pivot board.
5. Glue small thread "cross hairs" across one end of a plastic straw. Glue the plastic straw to the top of the pivot board.

6. Cut the dowel and push it through the two vertical supports. It should extend about 1 cm beyond the outside of the support.
7. Drill a small hole through the extended ends of the dowel and push a 3 cm nail through. **This is your indicator for degrees of elevation.**
8. Place the pivot board on top of the dowel and using blocks to keep it level, glue it in place.

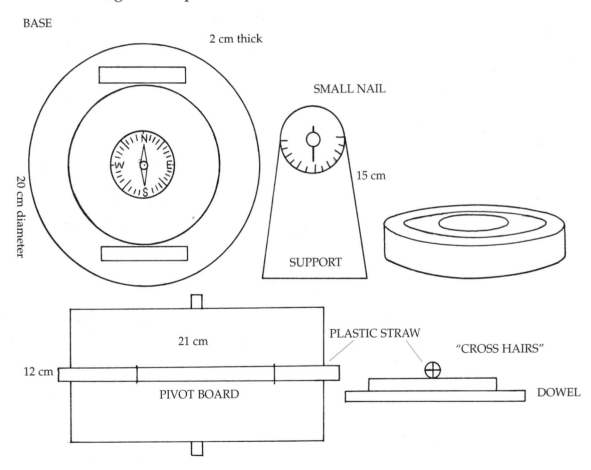

BASE

2 cm thick

SMALL NAIL

20 cm diameter

15 cm

SUPPORT

21 cm

12 cm

PLASTIC STRAW

"CROSS HAIRS"

PIVOT BOARD

DOWEL

Using the transit:

Place the transit on a **level** surface. (You may wish to make a tripod for it.) Sight an object by looking through the straw and fixing the "cross hairs" on it. The compass will indicate the **direction** of the object, the nail through the dowel will indicate the **angle of elevation** of the object. Practice recording these readings. With your transit and a measuring tape you can begin simple surveying.

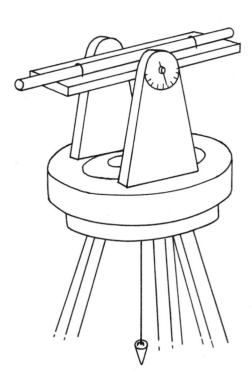

The Politicians

John A. Macdonald and Others

Politicians are frequently criticized today, and the same was true in the 1800s. But without their efforts, many exciting advancements might never have been achieved. Canada's first and most famous prime minister was Sir John A. Macdonald. He created the Dominion of Canada in 1867, and had the first Canadian coast-to-coast railway built by 1885.

Born in Glasgow, Scotland, in 1815, John Macdonald emigrated to Kingston in Canada at the age of five with his parents and three siblings. As the blue-eyed youth with black curly hair grew taller, his nose also grew to a large and prominent size!

Transportation in those times was slow and difficult, so young John had to board in Kingston to attend school there, although his home was only 45 km away at Glenora. He graduated from the District Grammar School at fourteen and went to work for a Kingston lawyer, George Mackenzie. By the time he was seventeen, he was running a branch office for Mackenzie in Napanee, about 40 km west. At twenty-one, he completed his studies to become an attorney and set up his own law practice in Kingston.

In 1841, the united province of Canada was created by the union of Upper Canada (present-day Ontario) and Lower Canada (present-day Quebec). Kingston became the capital city.

SIR JOHN A. MACDONALD

Macdonald was a natural politician. His love of drinking and talking with friends, his sense of humour, his memory for names and faces, his ability to flatter others, and his tough character all contributed to his political career. He never liked to make decisions in a rush and preferred to put them off until another day — hence his nickname, "Old Tomorrow."

In 1857, Macdonald became premier of the Province of Canada. In that same year his first wife, Isabella, died. In 1867, Macdonald, along with his right-hand man George Etienne Cartier and other supporters, created the new Dominion of Canada consisting of four provinces: Ontario, Quebec, New Brunswick, and Nova Scotia. One of the conditions of the formation of the new country was that an Intercolonial Railway be built to link the provinces together. For forming the new country, Macdonald was knighted. When he returned from England in 1867 with Canada's constitution, the British North American Act (BNA Act), he also brought with him a beautiful and healthy new wife, Susan Agnes Bernard, who was twenty-two years younger than he was.

On the Pacific Coast in faraway British Columbia, an unusual and eccentric politician who had chosen the name Amor de Cosmos, which means "Lover of the Universe," to replace his real name of Bill Smith, was suggesting that British Columbia become the fifth province. In 1871, he was successful. One of the conditions of B.C. joining Canada was that a railway that would link Canada to the new province had to be built across the continent within ten years.

While fighting for election in 1872, Macdonald relied heavily on campaign contributions from Sir Hugh Allan, who was to build the new Pacific Railway to British Columbia. When a telegram from Macdonald to Allan's lawyer on August 26, 1872, became public, it exploded in the newspapers and caused what became known as "The Pacific Scandal" leading to the humiliation and resignation of Sir John A. Macdonald. The telegram read:

I must have another ten thousand... Do not fail me.

Macdonald's political career seemed doomed, and the coast-to-coast railway was delayed until after a surprising election in 1878. The Liberal government of Prime Minister Alexander Mackenzie was defeated, and Macdonald once again became prime minister. He completed the Canadian Pacific Railway to British Columbia in 1885.

Sir John A. Macdonald remained the prime minister of the country he had created and joined together with railways until his death in 1891.

Charles Tupper

The Nova Scotia politician, Charles Tupper, who supported Macdonald's proposal to create the Dominion of Canada, was appointed the Minister of Railways in the new country.

Prince Edward Island Joins Confederation

In 1873, Prince Edward Island became the sixth province of Canada. One of the conditions was that the Canadian government take over the PEI Railway system.

Mysterious Train Stories

There are many strange stories told about Canadian trains.

The Headless Brakeman
There is the story of Hub Clark, the "Headless Brakeman" whose head was severed from his body by a locomotive when he was knocked unconscious on the tracks in the Vancouver yards in 1928. Many years later, people still claimed to see a headless figure haunting the site.

Strange Passengers

A Haitian porter on the Montreal–Toronto run described an eerie couple, both dressed in black, who boarded his train. Around Cornwall, the thin young man came screaming for assistance, and when the porter returned to the couple's compartment, the pale-faced woman was lying dead on the bed. Her husband fell to his knees in agony, swearing that he would do anything to save her. The porter ran to get the conductor, but when they returned, it was the man who lay dead on the bed and the confused young woman who sat on the floor staring at him.

Dream or Warning?

Freeman Prevoe, a brakeman on Nova Scotia's Intercolonial Railway, had been haunted by a recurring dream of a white horse on the railroad tracks in front of a locomotive. One stormy night on a run to Antigonish, he actually saw the white horse from his dreams on the tracks in front of his train. Prevoe feared that it was a warning of disaster but couldn't convince the engineer to believe him or pull the train onto a siding until the fierce storm was over. Later that night, in flooding rain, the train was swept off the tracks, killing the engineer and injuring the fireman, but Prevoe survived.

Ghost Train

The *Spokane Flyer*, with engineer Jim Nicholson, was running from Medicine Hat to Swift Current in 1908 when it smashed head-on into a Lethbridge passenger train with engineer Bob Twohey at the controls. Both engineers and five other people were killed in the tragedy.

Many years later in the 1930s, Gus Day, a fireman, revealed two strange experiences that he had witnessed at the exact spot where the trains collided. He and engineer Twohey, two months before the crash, had thought that they were about to die in a head-on collision when a bright light appeared on the tracks in front of them. But the approaching train whipped past them with its whistle screaming and passengers clearly visible in its coach cars. The "Ghost Train" was impossible to explain because there was only one set of tracks at that location. To add to the mystery, Day was later on another train, with Nicholson driving, when they experienced the same phenomenon, at the same spot, also in the middle of the night. The "Ghost Train's" light appeared in front of them, and again it roared past with whistle blasting and the passengers clearly visible in the illuminated coach cars. Both the dead engineers and Day had told close friends about the "Ghost Train" experience before the fateful disaster occurred.

The Mounties

Sir John A. Macdonald created a national police force called the Northwest Mounted Police (today known as the Royal Canadian Mounted Police) and sent the red-coated constables west to keep law and order. They had to control the natives, cowboys, immigrants, gold miners, farmers, whiskey traders, and railroad construction workers. Mounties not only arrested lawbreakers but held frontier courts that sentenced them. Mountie courts might be held in log cabins, tents, or even on wagon carts, but they were based on one law for the entire Northwest and all its inhabitants regardless of race or status. This was a very different system of justice from that in the United States to the south, where every town or territory elected sheriffs or marshals to enforce the dozens of laws determined by the local communities.

Runaways

The steep grades of the CPR in the Rocky Mountains and the lack of air brakes on trains in the 1880s made runaway trains a constant threat. To prevent trains from hurtling out of control when descending the steep mountain slopes, the CPR built sidings off the main tracks and stationed a worker at each switch. If an engineer felt that he was losing control of his train, he would blow his whistle. On hearing the shrill alarm, the switch-man would then switch the runaway onto the siding that sloped back up the side of the hill and ended in a large earth embankment. Usually the train would be stopped by the uphill slope rather than the wall of earth at the end of the siding.

40

Activity: Switching Puzzles

Switching Problems

The dining car on a first-class passenger train has a problem. The stoves are not working and can't be fixed en route. The dining car in the middle of the train must be replaced with a new one from the siding. How can this be done with the fewest moves backward and forward? (The answer is on page 89).

Following this example create switching problems of your own.

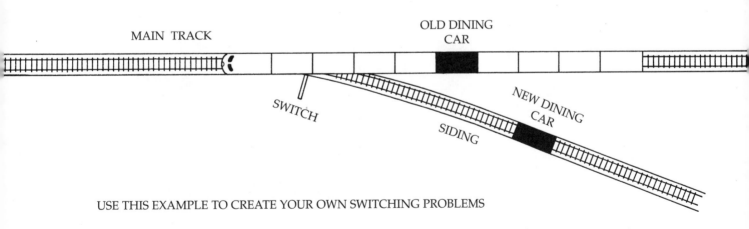

MAIN TRACK   OLD DINING CAR

SWITCH   SIDING   NEW DINING CAR

USE THIS EXAMPLE TO CREATE YOUR OWN SWITCHING PROBLEMS

GABRIEL DUMONT

The Opponents

Rebels, Natives and Rioters

Whenever a new invention is created, there will be people who accept and encourage it and others who will have doubts and try to prevent it. Although there were many famous Canadians who helped to build the railways, there were others who tried to stop this from happening — often for good reasons.

Of course, there were political opponents to the railways. One of these was Alexander Mackenzie who, while he was prime minister from 1872 to 1878, believed that Sir John A. Macdonald's dream of a transcontinental railway was "one of the most foolish things that could be imagined." He refused to proceed with it.

In the west were rebel Métis, such as Louis Riel who, in 1870, had led the Red River Rebellion in Manitoba. And guerrilla leader Gabrielle Dumont, nicknamed "the Prince of the Plains," who persuaded Riel to return from hiding in the U.S.A. where he had fled after the failure of the Manitoba rebellion. In 1885, Riel and Dumont led the Northwest Rebellion in Saskatchewan and Alberta.

The Métis told the native peoples that the railway would bring white settlers who would occupy the land, drive away the herds of buffalo and other game, and set fire to the prairies with the thundering black smokestacks that spit out fiery sparks and ashes from clouds of erupting steam.

All their predictions came true.

The native leaders of the prairie bands feared and distrusted the iron demon they called the "fire wagon." But when the grading and construction crews, numbering more than 5,000, arrived on the western plains in the early 1880s, the various native leaders responded in different ways.

Chief Poundmaker told his people: "The railway will be close to us, the whites will fill the country and they will dictate to us as they please." But he concluded that it was hopeless to try to stop it.

When the railway crews arrived at the Cypress Hills in the winter of 1882–83, a Cree chief, Piapot, sent his braves to uproot 64 km of railroad survey stakes, and pitched his camp on the railway right-of-way. Two scarlet-coated Northwest Mounted Police officers arrived on black horses and the corporal, William Brock Wilde, gave Piapot fifteen minutes to move the human roadblock. The native warriors threatened the two men but, when the time was up, Wilde dismounted, marched up to Piapot's tepee, and pulled it down on the heads of the women inside. He then proceeded through the Cree camp knocking down all of the buffalo-skin lodges. Admiring the courage of the young Mountie, Piapot ordered his followers to pick up their belongings and leave the railway lands.

The Methodist missionary, John McDougall, ensured that his native friends, the Stoneys, caused no trouble, and one Blackfoot chief, Crow Shoe, even greeted the workers as friends.

Chief Crowfoot reacted angrily when construction workers arrived on his Blackfoot reserve east of Calgary. The Canadian government had promised him the lands forever and signed a treaty, but then came to build a railway across his reserve. With over 700 warriors ready to attack, he confronted the railway crew until Father Albert Lacombe, a Roman Catholic missionary, used his friendship with Crowfoot to avoid bloodshed. The

chief agreed to let the railway continue in exchange for additional lands. To help keep the peace, businessman William Van Horne gave Crowfoot a free lifelong pass for the railway but, although the chief took trips on them, he remained suspicious and distrusted the trains.

The railway was most threatened when the Northwest Rebellion erupted in 1885 and the Crees, under Chief Big Bear, joined forces with the Métis leaders to attack the white settlers at Frog Lake. The army, Mounties, and special units, such as the Rocky Mountain Rangers, had to protect the railway line near Medicine Hat from native attacks. William Van Horne promised to transport thousands of Canadian volunteer and militia army troops from Toronto to Fort Qu'Appelle in Saskatchewan territory. He transferred them in only nine days. Before the railway, during the first Riel rebellion in Manitoba, it had taken Canadian troops from Toronto three months to reach Fort Garry. The rebels were defeated; the grateful government came to Van Horne's financial rescue. The railway was completed to the Pacific Ocean.

At times, the railroad workers themselves threatened the completion of the line. By 1884, the famous Inspector Sam Steele of the Northwest Mounted Police established an advance headquarters at the frontier railway town of Beavermouth, west of Kicking Horse Pass. There was a 16 km "no trespassing zone" around the railroad construction, but outside the line a wild boom town had developed. Merchants, saloonkeepers, dance hall women, and gamblers crowded into town to prosper from the wages of the railroad workers.

On April 1, 1885, a mob of furious railway workers went on strike because they had not received their wages for several months. Although 1,200 men joined the strike, non-striking workers continued to lay the tracks. Three hundred rioters with guns tried to stop a trainload of workers but the boss, James Ross, drove the locomotive through the strikers with bullets whizzing past his ears.

Sam Steele, very ill and confined to his bed, could only spare four Mounties to protect the workers, but he sent Sergeant Billy Fury to confront the hundreds of angry, shouting strikers who were firing their guns into the air. Fury's threat to shoot anyone who tried to pass his small detachment of men caused the rioters to retreat back to Beavermouth.

By the time Fury reported back to Steele in his sick bed, another problem had erupted. A Mountie trying to arrest a suspect in the shanty-town had been attacked. Steele sent Fury and his men to make the arrest; Fury disappeared into the boom town and then a shot was heard. Steele crawled to the window of his cabin to see the four constables with their prisoner being pursued by a threatening gang of workers. Ignoring his illness, Steele grabbed his rifle and rushed out to defend his men. Warning the mob to keep their hands off their guns, he had an assistant read the Riot Act that gave Steele the official authority to use any force necessary. As eight Mounties cocked their rifles behind him, he warned the strikers that he would open fire on any group of 12 or more who assembled in public. The rioters dispersed.

The railway paid the overdue wages, but the ringleaders of the riot were fined $100 or given six months hard labour.

Death on the Rails

Riding on early Canadian trains was dangerous, and sometimes deadly. The GWR had nineteen accidents in 1854, its first year of operation. On October 27, fifty-two people were killed and forty-eight injured near Chatham, Ontario. On March 12, 1857, a Toronto-Hamilton express train suffered a broken wheel or axle, was derailed, and fell into the Dejardins Canal killing sixty people. The worst accident in Canadian railway history occurred at Beloeil, Quebec, on June 28, 1864, leaving ninety people dead.

Working on the early railways was also hazardous. In only six years, thirty-eight CPR surveyors died from starvation, forest fires and other accidents in the wilderness. Tunnel deaths were frequent, especially when dynamite explosions hurled large boulders from the mouths of the tunnels. Many workers fell to their deaths from the steep canyon walls of the Rocky Mountains. Avalanches of mud and snow, floods, and prairie grass fires all claimed victims.

Railway work was the most hazardous industrial occupation in Canada in the early twentieth century. The development of air brakes, automatic coupling of cars and better signals gradually reduced the dangers to railway workers and travellers.

Bridge of Death

When it was being built in the early 1900s, the Quebec Bridge was the world's largest cantilevered bridge. Connecting Quebec City with the south shore of the St. Lawrence River, this bridge took seventeen years to complete. While under construction on August 29, 1907, part of the bridge collapsed, killing seventy-five workers. On September 11, 1916, while the final span was being placed in position, it fell and killed another ten men. Finally, on October 17, 1917, the first train crossed the structure safely.

Jumbo Disaster

When you eat a "Jumbo" ice cream cone or hamburger, or travel on a "Jumbo" jet, you may not realize that the word came from Jumbo, the African elephant. Captured in Kenya and shipped to a zoo in London, England, Jumbo became known world-wide as the largest elephant in captivity.

After P.T. Barnum of the Barnum and Bailey Circus purchased the gentle, friendly Jumbo, the elephant's fans in Britain were outraged. But Barnum refused to sell back his prize. Thousands lined the waterfront and streets of New York when Jumbo arrived in the U.S.A. Jumbo toured North America by rail in his own circus "Palace Car."

In 1885, at St. Thomas, Ontario, as Jumbo was crossing the tracks to return to his "Palace Car" after a performance, an unscheduled Grand Trunk train appeared unexpectedly out of the fog. The locomotive and two cars were derailed; Jumbo was killed. A life-size statue of Jumbo was built in St. Thomas one hundred years later, in 1985, in honour of the large accident victim.

49

Race to the Pacific Board Game

What You need:

>   scissors
>   a small piece of cardboard
>   a paper fastener
>   coins or small stones

What to do:

1. Following the example on the following page, draw a circle. Divide it into four parts. Draw an arrow with a circle in the centre.
2. Cut out the circle and arrow.
3. Make a hole in the centre of each and push a paper fastener through the two pieces and attach them. You now have a spinner for playing the game.
4. Use coins or small stones as game counters.

How to play:

1. Spin the spinner to see which player moves first. The winner may choose the Northern or Southern Route.
2. Each player in turn spins and moves the number of places indicated. Check the Northern Route's and Southern Route's charts for special

instructions on any of the marked circles. Examples: move ahead; lose a turn, etc.

3. When approaching the Pacific, you must spin the correct number to land directly on the Finish Circle. You may spin only once each turn. The first player to reach the Pacific wins.

4. For a longer game you may return to the East Coast. Ignore the "see chart" signs. Your railway is complete. You may use the bridges and tunnels to save time.

Play Charts for the Board Game
Northern Route Chart

2- Build bridge — move ahead to 5
7- Funding cut off — lose one turn
12- Unpaid workers go on strike — lose one turn
15- Good weather, dry ground — move ahead one space

Southern Route Chart

6- Supply of rails delayed — lose one turn
8- Dig tunnel — move ahead to 11
13- Good progress — move ahead one space
16- Natives block right-of-way — lose one turn.

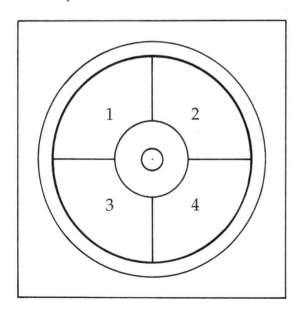

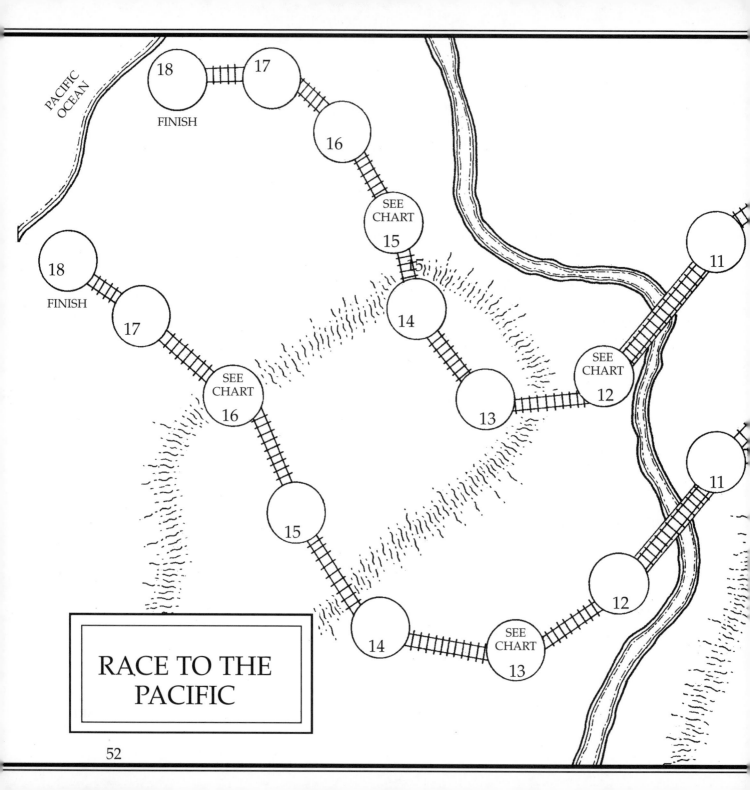

PACIFIC OCEAN

18 FINISH

17

16

SEE CHART 15

14

15

11

SEE CHART 12

13

18 FINISH

17

SEE CHART 16

15

14

11

12

SEE CHART 13

RACE TO THE PACIFIC

52

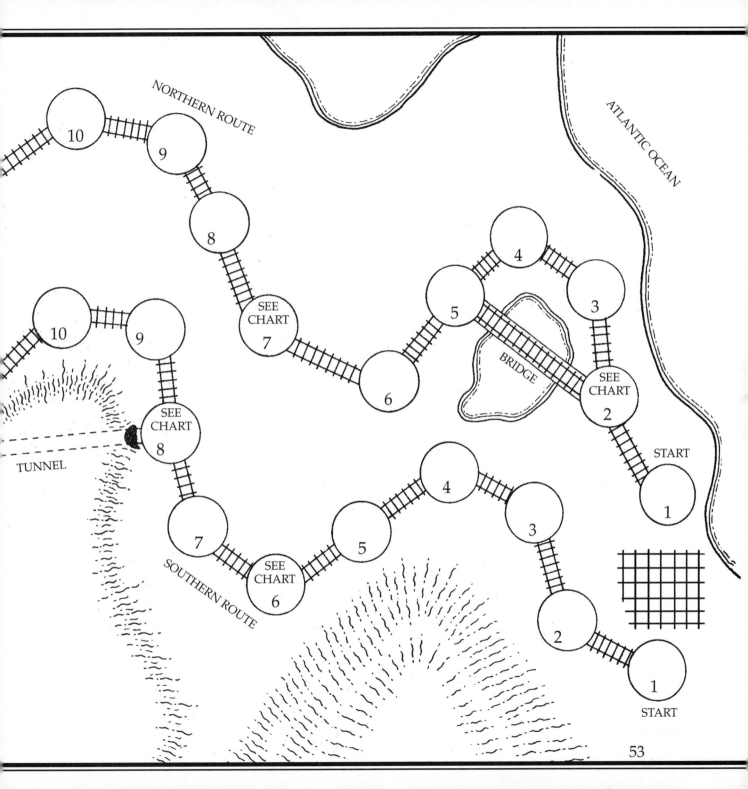

NORTHERN ROUTE

ATLANTIC OCEAN

10

9

8

SEE CHART 7

6

5

4

3

SEE CHART 2

START 1

10

9

SEE CHART 8

TUNNEL

7

SEE CHART 6

SOUTHERN ROUTE

5

4

3

2

START 1

BRIDGE

53

The Businessmen

William Van Horne and Others.

Building and running railways was a business. If early railroad companies were to be successful, they had to have outstanding business people in charge.

In the mid 1800s, the expanding and prosperous young country of Canada attracted new citizens from many parts of the world, including the U.S.A. William Van Horne, born on February 3, 1843, in Chelsea, Illinois, was one such immigrant.

William's father, who was a lawyer, politician, and associate of Abraham Lincoln, died suddenly of cholera when the boy was only eleven years old. Because of the large debts owed by his father, the family was instantly poor. To help his mother buy food for the family, William found a job delivering telegrams — and became intrigued with the early science of telegraph communications.

At school, William was an active and lively youth who would never back away from a physical fight. He also had a creative and imaginative mind and used his artistic talents to draw caricatures of his classmates and teachers. One day he was caught with a cartoon version of his principal. The furious principal dragged the boy to his office and beat him severely with a cane that he kept for disciplining students. William, fourteen, quit school that day and decided to educate himself.

WILLIAM
VAN HORNE

At fourteen, William obtained a job as a telegrapher for the Illinois Central Railway Company in Chicago, but it ended abruptly because of the youth's love of playing practical jokes. He ran a live electrical wire from his boss's office to a steel plate in the railway yards and, watching from the window, he giggled mischievously when workers who stepped on the plate recoiled in terror as they received an unexpected shock. Electricity was a new and relatively unknown science, so the puzzled workers were unable to discover the source of their discomfort. Unfortunately, William's boss, who did understand electricity, became an unwitting victim. The angry boss fired the boy instantly.

William's next job was as a freight-checker and messenger for the Michigan Central Railway in Joliet for fifteen dollars a month. When the General Superintendent visited the railway yards, travelling in his private railway car, eighteen-year-old William was awed. He vowed to attain such a position himself one day. Ten years later, William Van Horne, at twenty-eight, became a general superintendent. Van Horne quickly moved from administration to construction.

The population of Canada at that time was only four million people but the estimated cost of a transcontinental railway was one hundred million dollars. A group of rich businessmen met with Prime Minister John A. Macdonald and agreed to complete the railway with the help of the Canadian government. The government agreed to give them the existing tracks, over ten million hectares of land, and twenty-five million dollars.

When the "CPR Syndicate" was formed in February of 1881 by Donald Smith, George Stephen, Duncan McIntyre, and James Hill, Hill insisted that William Van Horne be the new general manager of the Canadian Pacific Railway.

Crossing the Western Plains

When the energetic Van Horne arrived in Winnipeg and started work in January 1882, progress on laying track escalated immediately. Using over 5,000 men and 1,700 teams of horses, he astonished everyone by completing 942 km of track west of Winnipeg in the first season. One of his senior engineers described him as "a great man with a gigantic intellect, a generous soul and an enormous capacity for food and work."

Van Horne continued to spread his tracks across the prairies but ran into conflict with his old supporter, James Hill, in Northern Ontario. The "CPR Syndicate" planned to link the Canadian railway with Hill's American one at Sault Ste. Marie, proceed through the U.S.A., and join up with the CPR at Winnipeg. Van Horne objected, saying, "Using Mr. Hill's line plainly puts the CPR at his tender mercies."

It was ironic that the American-born Van Horne was promoting a Canadian route, yet Hill, from Galt, Ontario, wanted to use his American route. Prime Minister John A. Macdonald agreed that the entire railroad should stay on Canadian soil, which resulted in Hill resigning his directorship and vowing: "I'll get Van Horne if I have to go to hell for it and shovel coal."

The "Big Hill"

After crossing the western prairies, Van Horne's workers encountered the last and greatest obstacle to completing a transcontinental railway — the towering Rocky Mountains.

At the "Big Hill" in Kicking Horse Pass, James Ross was in charge of building 7.25 km of track on an impossible 4.5 percent grade between Wapta Lake and the bottom of Mount Stephen. The powerful locomotives had eight driving wheels, twice as many as typical engines of the time, to climb such a steep slope. But the real danger was runaways when they tried to descend the other side.

Mountain Creek Bridge

Having conquered the "Big Hill," James Ross came to the east side of the Selkirk Mountains where he built the Mountain Creek Bridge, over 48 m high and 325 m long. On the west side, he created a series of loops to overcome the steep slope.

From the West

On the West Coast, the man in charge of building the railway through the Fraser Canyon to link up with the tracks coming from the east, was a wealthy American businessman, Andrew Onderdonk. He wore the same elegant clothing in the wild and muddy mountain boom town of Yale as he did in his sophisticated home city of New York.

He had an almost impossible job. The rivers were fast and treacherous; the mountains were high and dangerous. He had to blast twenty-seven tunnels through the mountains and build over 600 trestles or bridges across rivers and canyons from Port Moody to Eagle Pass. Onderdonk's crews worked at altitudes as high as 1,600 m. To carve a route along the rocky sides of mountains, the men went barefoot as they were lowered on the ends of ropes to drill holes in the rock, set dynamite charges and then scramble frantically up to safety before the explosion. The native Indians gained the reputation of the most fearless and best rock workers at high altitudes.

Many workers died from flying rocks, collapsing tunnels, the careless use of explosives, and unexpected avalanches of snow, mud, and rock.

Progress was slow as they averaged less than two m a day; nevertheless, Onderdonk's crews reached Eagle Pass, the place where the eastern workers were to link up with them, five weeks before the others.

Skuzzy

The steep canyon walls of the whirling Fraser River killed many railroad construction workers. The Canadians called it "Hell's Gate"; the Chinese labourers named it "The Slaughter Pen."

In 1882, Andrew Onderdonk built a river boat called the Skuzzy to bring supplies up the Fraser River through "Hell's Gate." After several failures, he finally succeeded by pounding ring-bolts into the rocky sides of the canyon, running heavy ropes attached to the ship through them, and using 150 Chinese workers to pull on the ends of the ropes along the riverside. In this fashion, Skuzzy brought supplies up river for the next year.

Rogers Pass

When Van Horne took charge of completing the railway to the west coast, he wanted the fastest route. But the Selkirk Mountains, 3,350 m high, stood in his way. He hired a rough-spoken, tobacco-chewing mountain surveyor from the U.S.A., Major A.B. Rogers, who spent two years searching the unknown mountains, cold glaciers, canyon walls, and deep valleys until he discovered a possible route that today is called Rogers Pass. Van Horne sent Sandford Fleming to confirm the finding. Fleming reported that it would be very difficult, but possible.

When the CPR sent Rogers a $5,000 cheque for his discovery, he never cashed it. Instead, he hung it on his wall as a souvenir; he was not interested in money, only the challenge of conquering the Selkirks.

Double Funeral

The mountain trestles in British Columbia were an awesome sight. On one occasion when a fearful engineer refused to drive his locomotive over a tall, fragile trestle, Van Horne jumped into the cab and grabbed the controls. The reluctant engineer then changed his mind, claiming: "If you ain't afraid of getting killed, with all your money, I ain't afraid either."

Van Horne promptly replied, "We'll have a double funeral — at my expense of course."

The locomotive proceeded to pass safely over the trestle.

Racing Locomotives

Frequently in the early years, the tracks of two competing railroads would run side by side for long distances — and engineers fell into the habit of racing their rivals. The challenge of getting to the destination before your opponent became part of the railway tradition, but it was never official policy.

Spiral and Connaught Tunnels

In 1909, the unique Spiral Tunnels were built west of Kicking Horse Pass. As trains snake their way up or down the side of the mountain, a locomotive emerging from a tunnel is able to see its own caboose, travelling in the opposite direction, entering the mouth of another tunnel. In 1916, the eight km-long Connaught Tunnel was cut through the Selkirk Mountains to eliminate the dangerous Rogers Pass line.

Dynamite Factories

It was necessary for the railroad builders to create their own dynamite factories along certain parts of the route to save the time and money of importing the dynamite. Van Horne built three of them as he blasted his way through the hard granite bedrock north of Lake Superior.

Andrew Onderdonk's second-in-command, Michael Haney, managed the western line and also established a dynamite factory in the wild boom town of Yale in the Rocky Mountains of British Columbia. At Yale it was not unusual for balls or parties to last a week; on two occasions, disastrous fires destroyed more than half the town. When Haney's dynamite factory at Yale exploded unexpectedly and damaged every building in the town, he merely built another one.

Chinese Labourers

It was Andrew Onderdonk who imported over 6,000 labourers in ten over-crowded ships from the Chinese province of Kwangtung. In 1880, there were only 35,000 citizens in British Columbia, and Onderdonk needed more than 10,000 workers to build the western section of the railway. He hired the oriental labourers through Chinese companies.

It was the dream of each oriental worker to save $300 which would allow him to return home a very rich man. Of the first 2,000 Chinese to arrive in 1881, 200 died immediately of scurvy. Because the "coolies" dressed differently, ate differently, and spoke a strange language, they were often ignored or discriminated against by the other workers. The Chinese tended to keep to themselves in huts built along the tracks, eating a diet of rice and salmon boiled in large pots. Since they had to pay for their food and shelter, it was unusual for a man to save more than $50 a year from his low wages. Most didn't even earn the passage home; the Chinese companies abandoned them once they reached Canada. More than 5,000 never returned to China, but, since they had not been allowed to bring wives or families with them, there are few descendants left in Canada today.

Railroad Nicknames

Railway names were usually shortened to their main initials, but imaginative passengers began creating their own "nicknames" based on the initials and the reputations of the lines.

Railway Name	Initials	Nicknames
ALGOMA CENTRAL & HUDSON'S BAY	AC&HB	"ALL CURVES & HARD BUMPS"
ONTARIO, SIMCOE & HURON	O,S&H	"OATS, STRAW & HAY"
PACIFIC GREAT EASTERN	PGE	"PRINCE GEORGE EVENTUALLY"
TORONTO TRANSIT COMMISSION	TTC	"TICKETS, TRANSFERS & CHAOS" or in later years "TAKE THE CAR"
TORONTO, HAMILTON & BUFFALO	T,H&B	"TO HELL & BACK"
WHITE PASS & YUKON RAILWAY	WP&YR	"WAIT PATIENTLY & YOU'LL RIDE"

Speeding Silk Trains

In the early 1900s, mysterious silk trains had the right of way over all other trains as they rushed at speeds of 145 km an hour from Vancouver, British Columbia, to the silk warehouses of New York City and Montreal.

The silk was used mainly to make women's stockings, rare and expensive items at the time. Because the cargo of raw silk was so valuable (a silk train with 21 cars had a cargo value of seven million dollars), railway police, armed with pistols, protected each train. Because the cargo was very perishable, saving every possible minute became a tradition; all other trains were sidetracked as the silk specials roared past them.

Like pampered racing cars, the silk trains stopped every 242 km for lubrication of their running gear to avoid overheating due to the high speeds, and also for a change of engines and crew.

Considering their reckless speeds, there were surprisingly few accidents associated with the silk trains. The most serious one occurred in the Fraser Canyon of British Columbia in 1927 when several cars flew off the tracks and plunged into the Fraser River, spilling their valuable bales of silk into the rushing waters.

The sealed silk trains did not always carry silk. Some special trains from 1917 to 1918 had a human cargo of Indo-Chinese labourers arriving from the Orient. They were to be transported from Vancouver to Halifax, loaded onto ships and sent across the Atlantic Ocean to work behind the allied army trenches in France during World War I. A total of 48,708 workers were secretly and safely transported in this fashion during the war.

NEW IMMIGRANTS WAITING FOR PASSAGE WEST

Land Boom

When Van Horne was planning his railway across the prairies west of Winnipeg, many people tried to predict what route it would take and where the future railway towns would spring up. They purchased large sections of land in the hope of making a fast profit by selling them back to the railway or future citizens of the towns. This caused land prices to increase to outrageous amounts, but the land boom only lasted a year. Some speculators made large profits; others lost fortunes.

Sink Holes

Section Fifteen of the CPR was north of Lake Superior where, in addition to the hard granite that had to be blasted away, there was another unusual natural obstacle, the mysterious muskeg. This strange soil appeared firm and normal, but beneath the moss and peat surface lurked large sink holes, sometimes 30 m deep, that would unpredictably swallow up any weight placed on top of them. On one occasion, three locomotives and many kilometres of completed rails disappeared, sucked down to a swampy grave beneath the deceptive muskeg.

Immigrant Engineer

Canada is a country founded by immigrants from many different countries who have participated in its development. A brilliant Polish immigrant, Sir Casimir Gzowski, engineered the Grand Trunk Railway and was largely responsible for its success.

T H E   G R O W T H   O F

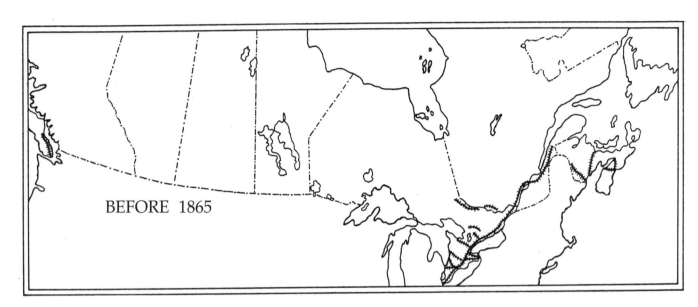

BEFORE 1865

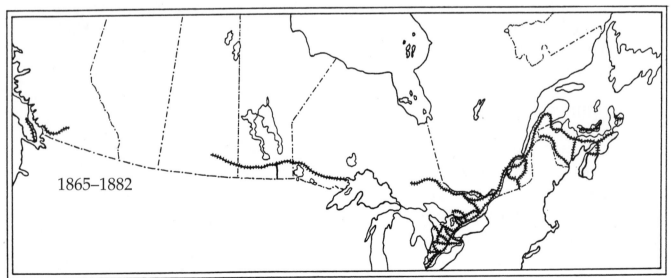

1865–1882

CANADIAN RAILWAYS

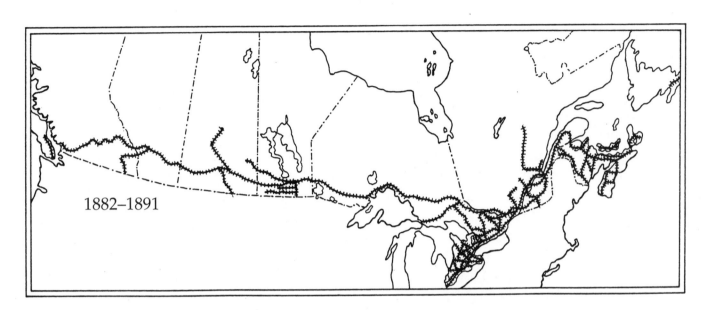

1882–1891

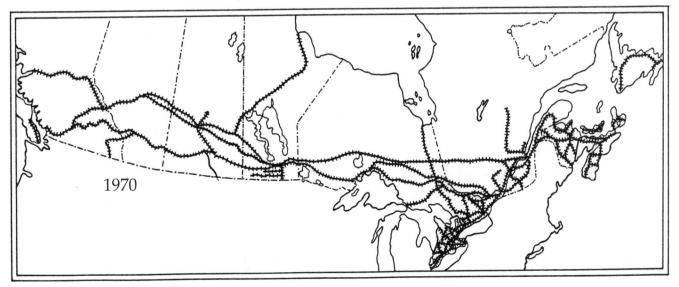

1970

Expanding Railways

The **Great Western Railway** (GWR) was quick to initiate new ideas. In 1854, it started the first on-train mail sorting. In 1858, it introduced the first sleeping cars for passengers. Its tracks spread from Niagara Falls in Canada West (Ontario) to Windsor with branch lines from: Hamilton to Toronto, Harrisburg to Galt, Komoko to Sarnia. GWR built the London, Huron and Bruce Railway in 1875 from London to Wingham.

The **Canadian Northern Railway** was created in 1896 when two western Canadian businessmen, William Mackenzie and Donald Mann, purchased the Lake Manitoba Railway and Canal Company. On January 23, 1915, the CNR became Canada's second transcontinental railway with over 16,000 km of track. It crossed the Rocky Mountains at Yellowhead Pass in Northern B.C., — the original route recommended for the CPR by Sandford Fleming, until Van Horne took over and insisted on a shorter southern route at Kicking Horse Pass.

When Sir Wilfrid Laurier was prime minister from 1896 to 1911, Canadian railways expanded tremendously. Those were prosperous times. Canada's population almost doubled as millions of immigrants arrived, lured by the government's offer of free land on the Prairies. Both the new Canadian Northern Railway, based in western Canada, and the pioneer Grand Trunk, based in eastern Canada, wanted to build railways across Canada to rival the existing CPR. Times were so good that Laurier allowed both railways permission and his government advanced money and land grants for the projects.

The **White Pass & Yukon Railway**, which runs from Skagway, Alaska, in the U.S.A. to Whitehorse, Yukon Territory, in Canada, is the most northerly railroad on the North American continent.

The **Pacific Great Eastern Railway** (PGER) was first established in 1912. It built the highest bridge in Canada (95.1 m) over Deep Creek, north of Williams Lake. In 1972 it became British Columbia Railways and in 1984 it was renamed again to B.C. Rail.

The **Canadian National Railway** (CNR) is today the largest railroad system in the world. World War I and the economic downturn of 1913 had forced the Grand Trunk and Canadian Northern railways into bankruptcy. After the war, the government decided to merge many of the existing railroads into one government-owned Canadian National Railway system. When it first came into existence on January 30, 1923, it amalgamated several historical Canadian railways including the Intercolonial in the Maritimes, the National Transcontinental, the Canadian Northern, the Grand Trunk and the Grand Trunk Pacific. It continued to acquire or build branch lines such as the Great Slave Railway (GSR) in 1965, which ran from Alberta to the Northwest Territory. Its motto was "Serves All Canada" because, at one point, it operated in every Canadian province, including Newfoundland and Prince Edward Island.

Radial Railways: In many parts of Canada, electric locomotives were used. These were called "radial" railways because they "radiated" out from a larger community to smaller ones; in the U.S.A., they were called "interurbans." The last radial railway in Canada to carry passengers was the Niagara, St. Catharines, and Toronto, in 1959.

Rapid Transit Lines and Subways: Today millions of Canadians travel to work, school, shopping and home on rapid transit lines and subways. Western Canadian cities like Vancouver, Calgary, and Edmonton have electric railways linking suburban communities with city centres. Toronto has electric trains running underground in its subway. Montreal has electric railways for commuters, and the only rubber-tired subway system in Canada.

Commuter Railways: Tens of thousands of Canadians use commuter trains every day. These services, usually owned and controlled by provincial and regional authorities, relieve highway congestion and urban pollution by transporting people quickly and efficiently into metropolitan centres from communities that can be 50 km away.

LRCs: Especially built for service throughout the Quebec City–Windsor "Corridor," the small but fast "LRCs" (for Light, Rapid, Comfortable) are Canadian designed and built trains operated by VIA Rail and featuring ultra-modern, streamlined locomotives and cars.

Shakespeare Line

In British Columbia, the Kettle Valley Railway (KVR) that ran through the Coquihalla Pass became known world-wide as an astonishing engineering accomplishment because of the hazardous mountains it had to overcome. In addition, it became a tourist attraction because of the unique names of its stations. Andrew McCulloch, chief engineer of the line, was a great fan of William Shakespeare and named all the stations, except for Coquihalla, after characters from famous Shakespearian plays, such as: Juliet, Romeo, Othello, Lear, Jessica, Portia, Iago.

This line was also the site of the famous "Quintette Tunnels." To reduce costs and travelling time, Andrew McCulloch bored five consecutive tunnels through the Coquihalla canyon. Two bridges were used to connect three of them. Today, visiters can stand at the mouth of one tunnel and look straight through the five, all in a straight row.

74

Identifying Engines

Steam locomotives were identified by their wheel arrangements. The smaller front wheels were indicated by the first number (usually 2 or 4). The second number indicated the large driving wheels (4, 6, 8 or 10). The third number indicated trailing wheels (0, 2, 4). Below are some examples:

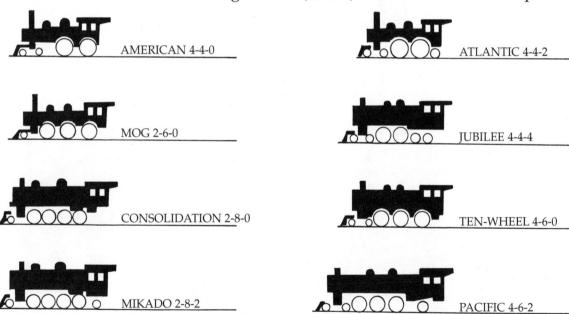

AMERICAN 4-4-0

ATLANTIC 4-4-2

MOG 2-6-0

JUBILEE 4-4-4

CONSOLIDATION 2-8-0

TEN-WHEEL 4-6-0

MIKADO 2-8-2

PACIFIC 4-6-2

Using this information, can you identify the engines on pages 4, 9, 45 and 59?

Jeanie, Lucy, Isabella and Susan

In the 1880s, women were not able to become surveyors, business people, or politicians, but that did not prevent them from influencing the men whom they loved or expressing their unique personalities and abilities.

Although concepts such as equality of the sexes or having the right to vote would not become popular until well into the 1900s, women were beginning to assert their independence and self-reliance. As adventurous young ladies insisted on journeying alone, the early train services encouraged them by having them met at the train station and escorted to special hotels that catered exclusively to female travellers.

Jeanie Hall

In 1845, Sandford Fleming met Jeanie Hall when he came to Peterborough, Ontario. They were immediately attracted to each other and became close friends.

Years later, as they were returning by sleigh from a trip to Toronto on a cold winter day in January, their vehicle rolled over, the horses ran in terror and Sandford's head was smashed against a tree stump, knocking him unconscious.

Jeanie dragged her friend through the snow to a farmhouse where she nursed his injuries until he was able to complete the trip to Peterborough. They were married a year later in 1855 and in the years from 1855 to 1861 became the parents of two sons and two daughters.

Lucy Hurd

In 1864, twenty-one-year-old William Van Horne encountered the beautiful Lucy Adaline Hurd, who was described as "tall, slender, and dignified, with softly waving black hair, hazel eyes and an apple blossom complexion." The nervous young William accidently stuffed a lit pipe into his jacket pocket, causing the pocket to burst into flames.

Three years later, the pair were married and moved into William's house. It soon became a busy one when William's mother and sister, as well as Lucy's mother, all came to live with them. The four women and William lived happily together and in 1868 a fifth female arrived, the Van Horne's newborn daughter, Adaline.

Tragedy struck in 1872 when Lucy caught the deadly smallpox. In those days the disease not only meant possible death or disfigurement, but the contamination of others. Patients were usually sent to be isolated in "pesthouses." However, William insisted on keeping Lucy at home, isolated in an attic room where he personally nursed her back to health, disinfecting himself before going to work. The disease did not spread to others and Lucy recovered completely.

Isabella Clark

In 1842, John A. Macdonald travelled to England and while visiting relatives on the Isle of Man was introduced to the charming and radiant Isabella Clark, his half-cousin, with whom he fell in love.

When Isabella came to visit mutual relatives in Kingston, Ontario, the next year, the couple were married within a few weeks. The poised Isabella was thirty-four; the love-stricken John was twenty-eight.

Within a year of the marriage, Isabella became ill. She had, in fact, become addicted to drugs. In the 1800s there were no illegal drugs. All forms of addictive medication were readily available and carried no warnings of their dangerous side effects. Many famous and intelligent people became victims before they realized the danger. John A. Macdonald himself became addicted to alcohol, which was a burden to him throughout his life.

Isabella gave birth to a healthy son in 1847, but the child died three years later. A second son was born in 1850 who was to live a full life, but Isabella became increasingly unhealthy and eventually a permanent invalid before her death in 1857.

Susan Agnes Bernard

Susan Agnes Bernard was the wife Macdonald brought back from England when he returned with the BNA Act in 1867 to establish the new Dominion of Canada. She provided the home, comfort, and companionship that had been missing in Macdonald's first tragic marriage. Some called her Macdonald's "Good Angel" because she had such a positive influence on him. He came to rely on her more and more as time passed.

Susan, twenty-two years younger than Sir John, was an adventurous companion. The two travelled west for the first time on the newly completed transcontinental railway, on a trip from Ottawa to the Pacific Coast. The Prime Minister's car, the *Jamaica*, was luxuriously furnished for the trip and it was greeted at every stop by enthusiastic westerners, including Chief Crowfoot.

When their train reached the awesome Rocky Mountains, Sir John preferred the comfort of the *Jamaica* but Susan rode the entire trip from

Laggan to the Pacific either in the cab of the locomotive or on the pilot or "cowcatcher." Her daring exploit set a fashion trend that other famous people of the time would later copy.

Although Sir John did join his wife for a brief time in Kicking Horse Pass, the First Lady was usually accompanied on the pilot by Joseph Pope, the prime minister's secretary.

In a letter to William Van Horne, Lady Macdonald described her adventure and an unexpected incident:

> I travelled on the Buffer beam from Laggan to Pt. Moody, every step of the way. Mr. Egan made me a lovely seat with a box and cushions, right in front of the Engine, and down the Kicking Horse Pass (we) flew on the big Engine in delightful style.
>
> Even among those wonderful loops near Rogers Pass, or on the sharp curves of the magnificent Fraser Canyon, so steady was the Engine that I felt perfectly secure and the only damage we did from Ottawa to the sea, was to kill a lovely little fat Pig, whom an error of judgement led under the engine near Nicomen, yesterday morning.
>
> I shut my eyes while he flew up and past, striking Mr. Pope who was sitting at my feet.

Tragedy struck Macdonald again in 1869 when Susan gave birth to a daughter, Mary, who turned out to be handicapped, both physically and mentally. Mary was never able to walk and remained confined to a wheelchair her entire life, unable to cope by herself because of her mental condition. Nevertheless, she lived until 1933, long after both her parents were dead.

Unique Canadian Trains

Fastest Passenger Train

The CPR's F-2-A locomotives (4-4-4) numbers 3000-3004, built in 1936, were the fastest passenger trains. They ran from Toronto to Montreal at a speed of 181 km/h. A new Canadian record was set in 1976 when the CNR's Turbo Train reached 226.2 km/h.

Slowest Passenger Train, *The Newfie Bullet*

The passenger train from St. John's to Port-aux-Basques was said to be so slow that the passengers could get off while it was running, go berry picking and get back on without being left behind.

Polar Bear Express

This train belongs to the Ontario Northland Railway and runs from Cochrane to Moosonee.

School on Wheels

From the 1920s to the 1960s special school trains visited the isolated northern communities of Canada. They would stop for a day or so on sidings where the travelling teachers would assign a week or two of homework to students before continuing to the next stop. There were also medical trains, with doctors and dentists, that visited the citizens of the remote Canadian north.

Modern Diesels

In 1928, the CNR 9000 was the first road diesel built in North America. By 1960, diesel locomotives had replaced the old steam engines. In 1990, the CNR received the first of the modern Dash 8-40 CM diesels built in Canada by General Electric.

Turbo Trains

The CNR operated Turbo Trains between Toronto and Montreal from 1974 to the early 1980s. Using jet turbines instead of diesel electric engines for power, these fast-moving, streamlined passenger trains were designed to roar around curves at speeds that would derail an ordinary locomotive or coach.

Prisoner-of-War Trains

During WWII, German prisoners captured in Europe were transported by rail to Canadian prisoner-of-war camps. Only one man ever escaped from the heavily guarded trains.

After being shot down on a raid over Britain, a German pilot, Franz Von Werra, was shipped to Canada. While being transported from Montreal to Ottawa, he dove headfirst from the coach window of a moving train in the

TURBO TRAIN

middle of a cold Canadian winter. From there, he made his way across the U.S. border to New York City, travelled to Rio, Brazil, and flew home to Germany, where Adolf Hitler personally welcomed him. The next year, 1941, he died on a mission when his plane crashed into the North Sea.

Largest Steam Engine
In the days of steam, railway competition was fierce as each company bragged about having the most powerful super locomotive. The CPR 8000 which operated from May 1931 to September 1936 was the largest. The last steam engine to be built in Canada was the CPR 5935 in 1949.

The Silver Streak
The *Canadian*, which has run between Montreal and Toronto to Vancouver since 1995, is the longest dome car ride anywhere. It has an ultra-modern shimmering stainless steel exterior and became a movie star when it was featured in a film called *The Silver Streak*.

Birth of the Canadian Broadcasting Corporation (CBC)

The CNR was the first railway in the world to have radio broadcasts for passengers' entertainment. During the 1920s, about fifty CN passenger trains were equipped with radio operators who monitored receiver sets while passengers wore headphones to listen to radio shows. CN operated eleven radio stations across Canada. These eventually came to form the basis of today's CBC.

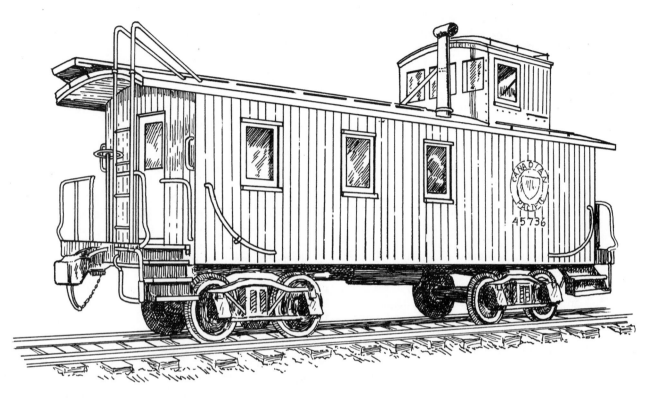

Disappearing History

Today, trains are still an important part of Canadian society. But the invention of the automobile and airplane brought some serious competition for both passengers and freight. In the provinces of PEI and Newfoundland, trains have disappeared completely. In many provinces, abandoned tracks have become hiking and snowmobile trails.

There are preserved locomotives, cars and stations in every province to remind us of the past. Canadians can still ride today on cars pulled by preserved steam locomotives.

Canadian Crossword Puzzle

ACROSS:

1. This famous Canadian company began as part of the CNR.
4. The person who shovels coal into the locomotive.
7. The place where a train is turned around.
11. Huge sink holes were caused by this obstacle.
14. Canada's second railway built in 1838.
15. The boss of a train crew.
16. The leader of the Red River Rebellion.
18. These special factories were built in the Rocky Mountains and Northern Ontario.
19. An African elephant killed by a GTR train in St. Thomas, Ontario.
20. Railway construction workers.
23. John A. Macdonald's handicapped daughter.
25. The first Canadian built locomotive ran on this railway.
27. Wooden planks on which railway tracks are laid.
31. He found a route through Kicking Horse Pass.
33. The Pass where the eastern and western sections of the tracks linked up to complete the CPR.
34. Nickname given to the Kettle Valley Railway Line.
37. John A. Macdonald's wife who became addicted to drugs and died.
38. He wanted the CPR to run through the U.S.A.
41. A railway boom town in the Rocky Mountains which was destroyed by a dynamite explosion.
42. These trains lost control and hurtled down the steep slopes of the Rocky Mountains.
43. A famous NWMP officer who kept law and order in the frontier railway towns.

DOWN:

1. Labourers were imported from this country to help build the CPR.
2. Small, fast, ultra-modern trains of VIA RAIL.
3. Largest railways system in the world.
5. Canadian PM who stopped the construction of the transcontinental railway from 1872 to 1878.
6. Métis leader known as "The Prince of the Plains."
8. This man was in charge of building the railway through the Fraser Canyon to link the east and west coasts.
9. Sharpened iron bars that secured the railway tracks.
10. Canada Police who kept law and order.
12. The width of a track.
13. Canadian PM who built the first transcontinental railway.
17. The person who hammered the last spike of the CPR.
19. The woman who saved Sandford Fleming after a sleigh accident.
21. American businessman who completed the CPR.
22. The locomotive on Canada's first railway in 1836.
24. These locomotives replaced the steam engines.
26. A blackfoot chief who received a lifelong pass on the CPR.
28. Special trains that travelled at high speeds.
29. These were constructed over rivers and gorges.
30. John A. Macdonald's "Good Angel."
32. A famous Canadian surveyor born in Scotland.
35. Crushed stone used to create a roadbed.
36. Used by Fleming to send a letter to his father.
39. This wife of William Van Horn recovered from smallpox.
40. North America's first attempted train robbery took place on this railway.

CANADIAN RAILWAY CROSSWORD PUZZLE

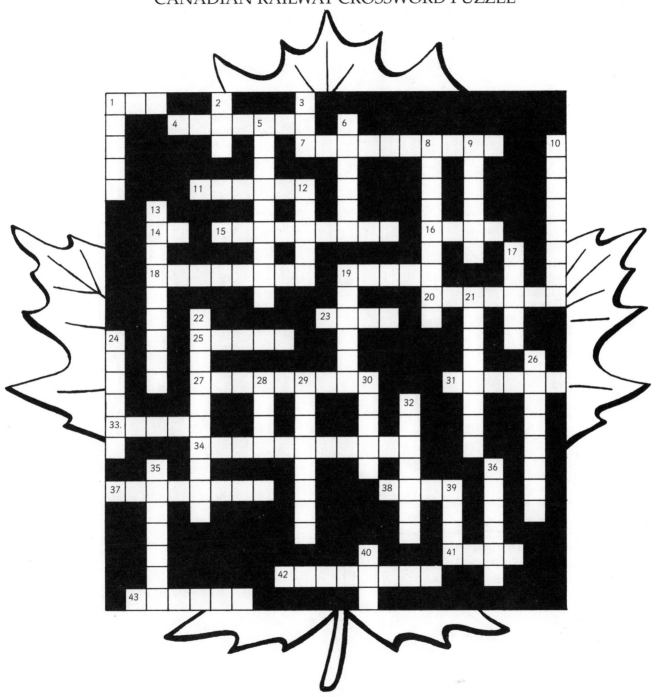

CANADIAN RAILWAY CROSSWORD PUZZLE ANSWERS

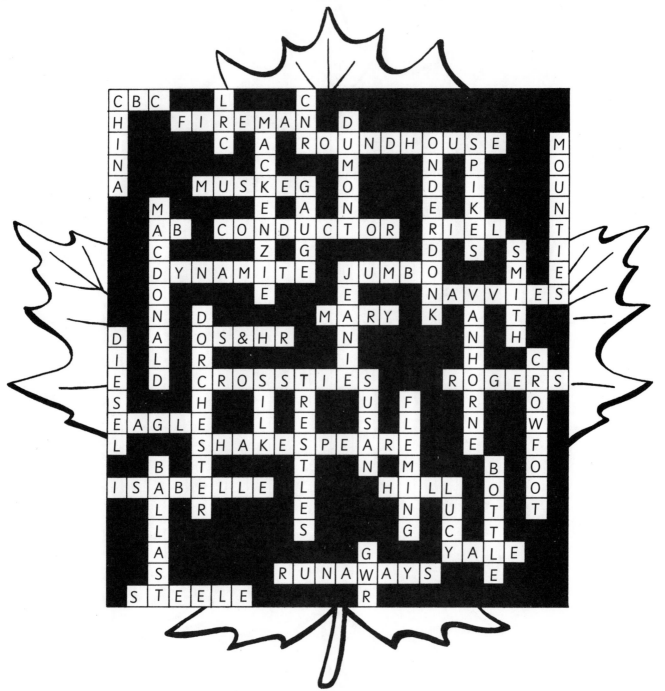

Answer to the switching problem on page 41.

1. The forward end of the train is uncoupled in front of the old dining car and moves forward (1) of the switch.
2. The forward end of the train backs (1) onto the siding and the new dining car is coupled.
3. The train moves forward (2) of the switch.
4. The train backs up (2) and the old dining car is coupled to the rear of the new one.
5. The train moves forward (3) of the switch.
6. The train backs up (3) onto the siding and the old dining car is left behind.
7. The train moves forward (4) of the switch.
8. The train backs up (4) and the new dining car is coupled to the rear of the train. The train is on its way and the passengers can be fed.

Index